YADA YAHUAH

BIBLICAL HEBREW

Learn to Read the Hebrew of the Scriptures
and Discover the Name Yahuah.

— ידע יהוה —

Levels 1 & 2

DR. YERAL E. OGANDO

Copyright

Yada Yahuah — Biblical Hebrew

Learn to Read the Hebrew of the Scriptures and Discover the Name Yahuah.

— ידע יהוה— Levels 1 & 2

 This course was developed to help students understand the Biblical Hebrew of the Scriptures and to provide direct access to the Hebrew text of the Tanak. The transliterations and linguistic explanations included in this course are presented for educational purposes and are designed to make the study of Biblical Hebrew accessible to students. The author recognizes that different academic approaches and traditions exist regarding the pronunciation of Biblical Hebrew. This course presents a specific

COURSE TITLE

Yada Yahuah — ידע יהוה— Biblical Hebrew

ISBN: 978-1-946249-42-5

First Edition: 2026

Language: English edition adapted from the original Spanish course

Printed and distributed for educational purposes.

TABLE OF CONTENTS

DEDICATION

This course is dedicated to all those who desire to approach the message of the Scriptures through its original language.

To the students who seek to understand Biblical Hebrew with humility, patience, and a sincere desire to learn.

To those who wish to read the Scriptures as closely as possible to the words in which they were originally transmitted.

And especially to those who desire to fulfill the purpose expressed in the name of this course:

ידע יהוה
Yada Yahuah

To know Yahuah.

INTRODUCTION

Biblical Hebrew is the language in which most of the Scriptures of the Tanak were originally written. Understanding this language allows the reader to approach the text of the Scriptures more directly, without relying solely on translations.

This course was designed to introduce students to the ancient Hebrew of the Scriptures by working with the consonantal text of the Tanak and with real words that appear throughout the biblical text.
The goal of this course is not only to learn a language, but also to gain a deeper understanding of the original message preserved in the Scriptures.
The name of this course reflects that purpose.

THE MEANING OF THE COURSE NAME

ידע — Yada

The word Yada means:

To know, to understand, or to perceive deeply.

In Biblical Hebrew, the word yada does not refer only to intellectual knowledge. It expresses a deeper kind of knowing — one that involves experience, understanding, and relationship.

יהוה— Yahuah

This is the Name of the Creator that appears thousands of times in the Scriptures.

The Name is formed by four Hebrew letters:

יהוה

Many modern translations replace this Name with titles such as "lord." However, in the original Hebrew text the Name appears clearly and repeatedly throughout the Scriptures.

HOW TO USE THIS COURSE

The course Yada Yahuah — ידע יהוה — Biblical Hebrew has been designed to guide the student step by step in learning the Biblical Hebrew of the Scriptures. The primary goal is to help the student recognize and understand the Hebrew text of the Tanak, beginning with the foundational elements of the language. This book contains the first two levels of the course, which establish the essential foundation required to begin understanding Biblical Hebrew.

STRUCTURE OF THE COURSE

Level 1 — Foundations of Biblical Hebrew

In this level the student will learn the basic elements of the language, including:

- The Hebrew alphabet
- Final letters (Sofit)
- First words from the Tanak
- Introduction to Hebrew roots
- Recognition of simple Hebrew words

The objective of this level is for the student to recognize the Hebrew letters and begin reading basic words from the Scriptures.

Level 2 — Structure of Biblical Hebrew

In the second level the student will learn important elements that appear constantly in the text of the Scriptures, such as:

- Common prefixes
- The definite article
- Important particles
- Frequently used Hebrew roots
- The plural in Biblical Hebrew
- Words that appear repeatedly in the Tanak

By the end of this level, the student will be able to identify many words within the Hebrew text of the Tanak and understand basic structures of the language.

LEARNING METHOD

Each lesson includes:

- Hebrew text
- Transliteration
- Word meanings
- Basic explanations
- Reading exercises

The course uses real words that appear in the Tanak so that students can become familiar with the language exactly as it appears in the Scriptures.

What Is the Tanak?

The word Tanak (תנ״ך) is an acronym formed from the three major sections of the Hebrew Scriptures.

SECTION	HEBREW	TRANSLITERATION
תורה	Torah	Instruction / Law
נביאים	Nabiym	Prophets
כתובים	Katubiym	Writings

The initials of these three words form the acronym:
תנ״ך
Tanak.

AUDIO PRONUNCIATION

All Hebrew words and expressions that appear in this course include an accompanying audio recording in MP3 format to help the student hear the pronunciation.

Download MP3 audio at www.aprendeis.com/download-mp3, choose your book title, and enhance your learning with audio.

Whenever the course presents:
• a Hebrew word
• a Hebrew phrase
• or a verse from the Tanak
the student will be able to listen to the corresponding audio and repeat the pronunciation.

The goal is not only for the student to recognize Hebrew words visually, but also to hear and practice the sounds of Biblical Hebrew.
Students are encouraged to listen to each audio several times and repeat the words aloud in order to become familiar with the sound of the language.
Consistent listening and repetition will greatly improve the student's ability to understand Biblical Hebrew.

RECOMMENDATIONS FOR THE STUDENT

To benefit fully from this course, it is recommended that the student:
• Study one lesson at a time
• Read the Hebrew words several times
• Listen to the pronunciation audio recordings
• Repeat the words aloud
• Regularly review previous lessons

Learning Biblical Hebrew requires patience and consistency. With regular practice, the student will begin to recognize many words directly within the biblical text.

THE PURPOSE OF THIS COURSE

The purpose of Yada Yahuah — **ידע יהוה** — Biblical Hebrew is to help students approach the original language of the Scriptures.
Through the study of Biblical Hebrew, the student can begin to understand more clearly the words that have been preserved in the Tanak.

In this way, learning the language also becomes a way of fulfilling the meaning expressed in the name of this course:
ידע יהוה
Yada Yahuah
To know Yahuah.

STUDENT PROGRESS

Yada Yahuah — **ידע יהוה** — Biblical Hebrew
This chart allows the student to track progress throughout the course.

It is recommended that each lesson be marked when:
- it has been read completely
- the exercises have been completed
- pronunciation has been practiced

LESSON PROGRESS

LESSON	TOPIC	COMPLETED
1	First Letters	☐
2	New Letters	☐
3	More Letters and First Roots	☐
4	New Letters and Biblical Words	☐
5	More Letters of Biblical Hebrew	☐
6	Final Letters of the Alphabet	☐
7	Roots of Biblical Hebrew	☐
8	Prefixes of Biblical Hebrew	☐
9	The Definite Article	☐
10	Final Letters (Sofit)	☐
11	Review of Lessons 1–10	☐
12	The Plural in Biblical Hebrew	☐
13	The Construct State	☐
14	Personal Pronouns	☐
15	Possessive Pronouns	☐
16	Fundamental Verb	☐
17	Word Order in Biblical Hebrew	☐
18	First Verse of the Tanak	☐
19	Frequent Words of the Tanak	☐
20	Foundational Roots	☐

ALPHABET PROGRESS

The student may mark each letter when he or she is able to recognize it easily inside words.

LETTER	NAME	MASTERED
א	Alef	☐
ב	Bet	☐
ג	Gimel	☐
ד	Dalet	☐
ה	He	☐
ו	Waw	☐
ז	Zayin	☐
ח	Het	☐
ט	Tet	☐
י	Yod	☐
כ	Kaf	☐
ל	Lamed	☐
מ	Mem	☐
נ	Nun	☐
ס	Samek	☐
ע	Ayin	☐
פ	Pa (pe)	☐
צ	Tsade	☐
ק	Qof	☐
ר	Resh	☐
ש	Shin	☐
ת	Taw	☐

VOCABULARY PROGRESS

HEBREW	TRANSLITERATION	MEANING	MASTERED
אב	Ab	Father	☐
בן	Ban	Son	☐
מלך	Malak	King	☐
מים	Mayim	Water	☐
ארץ	Arats	Earth / Land	☐
שם	Sham (Shem)	Name	☐
יום	Yom	Day	☐
אלהים	Alohiym	(gods)	☐
יהוה	Yahuah	Name of the Creator	☐
שמע	Shama	To hear / listen	☐

RECOMMENDATION FOR THE STUDENT

To progress more easily through the course, it is recommended that the student:

- study one lesson at a time
- listen to the pronunciation audios
- repeat the words aloud
- review the alphabet regularly
- practice reading Hebrew frequently

Steady progress will help the student recognize more and more words from the Tanak with confidence.

PRONUNCIATION GUIDE FOR HEBREW TRANSLITERATIONS

Yada Yahuah — ידע יהוה — Biblical Hebrew
This guide explains how to pronounce the Hebrew words that appear in transliterated form throughout this course.
The student should read the transliteration, not the Hebrew letters directly.

Example

YAHUAH (יהוה)

Pronunciation:

yah-hoo-ah

ALOHIYM (Elohiym) (אלהים)

Pronunciation:

ah-lo-heem

The pronunciation system of this course follows a simplified phonetic method designed to help students read Biblical Hebrew more easily.

NOTE ABOUT THE PRONUNCIATIONS USED IN THIS COURSE

In some Hebrew words in this course, two pronunciation forms may appear.

Example

ALOHIYM (Elohiym)

This means the following:

ALOHIYM

Represents the pronunciation system used in this course, based on an older form of Hebrew. This will always be the primary pronunciation used for teaching. (Elohiym)

Represents a more familiar modern or academic pronunciation. It is included only as a reference and will always appear in parentheses.

COURSE RULE

Whenever a word appears in this format:
OLDER FORM (modern form)

the student should:
1.Read the older course form.
2.Treat the form in parentheses only as a reference.

Example
אלהים

ALOHIYM (Elohiym)
Meaning: gods

EXAMPLES USED IN THIS COURSE

HEBREW	COURSE FORM	MODERN FORM
אלהים	ALOHIYM	(Elohiym)
ישראל	YASHARAL	(Yisrael)
בראשית	BARASHIT	(Bereshit)

1. VOWELS

Vowels in the Transliteration

The vowels in this course are pronounced consistently.
Ancient Biblical Hebrew was written mainly with consonants. The vowels were not originally written in the consonantal text and were preserved through oral transmission.

To make learning easier, this course uses Latin vowels in the transliteration system to help the student pronounce the words.
These vowels do not necessarily represent the exact original vocalization of ancient Biblical Hebrew. They are used as a teaching aid to make reading easier.

VOWELS USED IN THIS COURSE

VOWEL	PRONUNCIATION	EXAMPLE
A	A	Father
E	E	Met
I	I	machine
O	O	Note
U	U	Rule

These vowels are used only in the transliteration, not in the Hebrew text itself.

Important Note

The original Biblical Hebrew text was written without vowels.

For this reason, the student should treat the vowels in the transliteration as a reading aid, not as part of the Hebrew word itself.

The vowels always keep the same sound in the course.

Examples

YAHUAH

yah-hoo-ah

YAHUSHA

yah-hoo-sha

2. MARKED VOWELS

In some transliterations, vowels may appear with marks or accents, for example:

Â

Ê

Î

Ô

Ĕ

These marks do not change the basic pronunciation for the student.

The vowel should still be pronounced the same way as the regular vowel.

Example

ÂLÔHÎYM

Pronunciation:

ah-lo-heem

3. THE LETTER H

When H appears inside a word, it is pronounced with a strong breathy sound.

Examples

WORD	PRONUNCIATION
YAHUAH	yah-hoo-ah
YAHUSHA	yah-hoo-sha
MASHIYACH	mah-shee-ahkh

Important Rule

If H appears at the end of a word, it is normally not pronounced.

Example

YAHUAH

Pronunciation:

yah-hoo-ah

4. THE SH SOUND

The combination SH is pronounced as sh.

This is the same sound heard in English words such as:

- show
- shampoo

Examples

WORD	PRONUNCIATION
YAHUSHA	yah-hoo-sha
MASHIYACH	mah-shee-ahkh

5. THE TS SOUND

The combination TS is pronounced together.

It is similar to the sound heard in the word pizza.

Examples

WORD	PRONUNCIATION
TSADOQ	tsa-doq
TSIYON	tsee-yon

6. THE CH / KH SOUND

In this course the combinations CH or KH represent a guttural sound produced in the back of the throat.

This sound does not correspond to the English "ch" sound as in the word church. Instead, it is a rough breathy sound produced deeper in the throat.

For many students, the easiest way to approximate this sound is to pronounce it like a stronger version of the English letter "H", produced from the throat.

How to Pronounce It

Try the following steps:

1. Start with the English H sound (as in house).
2. Then push the air from deeper in the throat.
3. Allow the sound to become slightly rough or breathy.

This produces a sound similar to:

- the Spanish J in José
- the German CH in Bach
- the Scottish CH in loch

Important Note

When you see CH or KH in the transliteration:

❌ Do not pronounce it like "ch" in church.

✓ Pronounce it like a strong breathy H coming from the throat.

Hebrew Letters Behind This Sound

This sound commonly represents the Hebrew letters:

ח — Het

כ — Kaf (without dagesh)

Both letters can produce this guttural "kh" sound in Biblical Hebrew pronunciation traditions.

Examples

WORD	PRONUNCIATION
CHANOK	kha-nok
MASHIYACH	mah-shee-ahkh

Practice

Say these words slowly:

CHANOK
kha-nok
MASHIYACH
mah-shee-ahkh

Focus on producing the sound from the throat rather than the front of the mouth.

7. THE NAME OF THE MOST HIGH

YAHUAH

Syllable separation:

YA — HU — AH

Pronunciation:

yah-hoo-ah

The final H is not pronounced.

8. The Title ALOHIYM

ALOHIYM (אלהים)

Pronunciation:

ah-lo-heem

9. Examples

TRANSLITERATION	PRONUNCIATION
YAHUAH	yah-hoo-ah
YAHUSHA	yah-hoo-sha
ALOHIYM	ah-lo-heem
YASHARAL	yah-sha-ral
MASHIYACH	mah-shee-ahkh

Recommendation for the Student

To learn pronunciation correctly:

- listen to the audio for each word
- repeat the words aloud
- practice each pronunciation several times

With steady practice, the student will be able to recognize and pronounce many Biblical Hebrew words.

THE COURSE TRANSLITERATION SYSTEM

Yada Yahuah —ידע יהוה — Biblical Hebrew

This chart shows how Hebrew letters are represented with Latin letters in this course.

The transliteration system is designed so that students can read Hebrew words easily through a clear and consistent pronunciation method.

Consonants

HEBREW	NAME	TRANSLITERATION	APPROXIMATE SOUND
א	Alef	A	vocal support / silent carrier
ב	Bet	B	B
ג	Gimel	G	G
ד	Dalet	D	D
ה	He	H	soft breathy H
ו	Waw	U / W	u / w
ז	Zayin	Z	Z
ח	Het	H	strong guttural H
ט	Tet	T	T
י	Yod	Y	Y / ee
כ	Kaf	K	K
ל	Lamed	L	L
מ	Mem	M	M
נ	Nun	N	N
ס	Samek	S	S
ע	Ayin	A	deep vocal sound

HEBREW	NAME	TRANSLITERATION	APPROXIMATE SOUND
פ	Pa (pe)	P	P
צ	Tsade	TS	ts
ק	Qof	Q	deep K
ר	Resh	R	R
ש	Shin	SH	sh
ת	Taw	T	T

FINAL LETTERS (SOFIT)

In Biblical Hebrew, five letters change their shape when they appear at the end of a word.

These special forms are called Sofit (final forms).
It is important to understand that these are not different letters.
They represent the same consonants as their regular forms.
The only difference is their position in the word.

When these letters appear at the end of a word, Hebrew uses the final (Sofit) form instead of the regular form.

REGULAR FORM	FINAL FORM	NAME
כ	ך	Kaf Sofit
מ	ם	Mem Sofit
נ	ן	Nun Sofit
פ	ף	Pa (pe) Sofit
צ	ץ	Tsade Sofit

IMPORTANT RULE

• Regular form → used at the beginning or middle of a word
• Final form (Sofit) → used only at the end of a word

Examples

WORD	TRANSLITERATION	MEANING
מלך	Malak	king
מים	Mayim	water
בן	Ban	son
אלף	Alaf	thousand
ארץ	Arats	earth

Example Breakdown

מלך

Letters:

מ — Mem

ל— Lamed

ך — Kaf Sofit

Even though the final letter looks different, it still represents the same consonant K as כ.

Why Hebrew Uses Final Forms

The final forms help make the structure of words easier to recognize when reading Hebrew text.

When you see one of these shapes, you immediately know the letter is at the end of the word.

Practice

Identify the final letters in these words:

מים

מלך

בן

ארץ

Try writing each word several times to become familiar with the final forms.

VOWELS USED IN THE TRANSLITERATION

Vowels Used in This Course

The transliteration system in this course uses simple, consistent vowel sounds. These vowels are pronounced in a stable way to help the student read Biblical Hebrew more easily.

They should not be read according to the many changing vowel sounds of English spelling.

VOWEL	APPROXIMATE SOUND	ENGLISH APPROXIMATION
A	Ah	like a in father
E	Eh	like e in met
I	Ee	like i in machine
O	Oh	like o in note
U	Oo	like u in rule

Y always pronounced like "ee"

Important Note

In this course:

- E is not pronounced like the English long ee in me
- I is not pronounced like the English i in bit or the long i in mine

Instead:

- E is pronounced eh
- I is pronounced ee

Examples

TRANSLITERATION	PRONUNCIATION GUIDE
YAHUAH	yah-hoo-ah
ALOHIYM	ah-lo-heem
YASHARAL	yah-shah-rahl
MASHIYACH	mah-shee-ahkh

Rule for the Student

When reading the transliteration:

- pronounce each vowel the same way every time
- do not switch to English-style vowel sounds
- follow the course pronunciation system consistently

The vowels always keep the same sound in the transliteration, even though the ancient Hebrew text itself did not originally include written vowels.

Special Combinations

COMBINATION	PRONUNCIATION
TS	Ts
KH	strong guttural sound (strong h)
CH	strong guttural sound (strong h)

Examples of Transliteration

HEBREW	TRANSLITERATION	PRONUNCIATION
יהוה	YAHUAH	yah-hoo-ah
אלהים	ALOHIYM	ah-lo-heem
ישראל	YASHARAL	yah-sha-ral
משיח	MASHIYACH	mah-shee-ahkh
ציון	TSIYON	tsee-yon

General Rule of the Course

Whenever a Hebrew word appears, the student should:

1. Read the transliteration
2. Listen to the audio
3. Repeat the pronunciation

This system allows any student to begin reading Biblical Hebrew even without previous knowledge of the language.

Important Note

Transliteration is a learning tool. It does not replace the Hebrew letters.

For this reason, each word in the course will appear in this order:

1. Hebrew text
2. Transliteration
3. Meaning

Example

מלך

Malak (melek)

King

HEBREW ALPHABET CHART

Yada Yahuah — ידע יהוה — Biblical Hebrew
Biblical Hebrew uses an alphabet of 22 letters.
Words are written from right to left.
Each letter has a traditional name and an approximate sound.

Hebrew Alphabet

LETTER	NAME	TRANSLITERATION	APPROXIMATE SOUND
א	Alef	A	pause or vocal support
ב	Bet	B	B
ג	Gimel	G	G
ד	Dalet	D	D
ה	He	H	soft breathy H
ו	Waw	W / U	w / u
ז	Zayin	Z	Z
ח	Het	H	strong guttural H
ט	Tet	T	T
י	Yod	Y	Y
כ	Kaf	K	K
ל	Lamed	L	L
מ	Mem	M	M
נ	Nun	N	N
ס	Samek	S	S
ע	Ayin	A	guttural / deep vocal sound
פ	Pa (pe)	P	P
צ	Tsade	TS	ts
ק	Qof	Q	deep K
ר	Resh	R	R
ש	Shin	SH	sh
ת	Taw	T	T

FINAL LETTERS (SOFIT)

Five letters change form when they appear at the end of a word.

REGULAR FORM	FINAL FORM	NAME
כ	ך	Kaf Sofit
מ	ם	Mem Sofit
נ	ן	Nun Sofit
פ	ף	Pa (pe) Sofit
צ	ץ	Tsade Sofit

Example of a Hebrew Word

מלך

Malak (melek)

King

This word includes three letters:

LETTER	NAME
מ	Mem
ל	Lamed
ך	Kaf Sofit

Recommendation for the Student

To become familiar with the Hebrew alphabet:

- look carefully at each letter several times
- read its name aloud
- listen to the pronunciation audio
- practice recognizing the letters inside Hebrew words

With steady practice, the student will begin to identify the Hebrew letters within the text of the Tanak more quickly and confidently.

YADA YAHUAH

BIBLICAL HEBREW

Learn to Read the Hebrew of the Scriptures
and Discover the Name Yahuah.

— ידע יהוה —

Level 1

LESSON 1 — FIRST LETTERS

Introduction

Biblical Hebrew is the language in which most of the Scriptures of the Tanak were originally written.

The first step in learning this language is becoming familiar with its alphabet. The Hebrew alphabet has 22 letters. Each letter has its own name and sound. In this first lesson, we will learn the first four letters and read our first words from the Tanak.

Lesson Objective

By the end of this lesson, the student will be able to:

- recognize the letters Alef, Bet, Gimel, and Dalet
- identify these letters inside Hebrew words
- read basic words from the Tanak

Alphabet Letters

HEBREW	NAME	READING
א	Alef	pause / vowel support
ב	Bet	B
ג	Gimel	G
ד	Dalet	D

Alef does not have its own sound like the other letters. It functions as a pause or support for a vowel.

EXPLANATION OF THE LETTERS

Alef — א

Represents a pause or glottal stop.

Example

אב

Ab (av)

Father

Bet — ב

Represents the sound B.

Example

בן

Ban (ben)

Son

Gimel — ג

Represents a hard G, as in:

- go
- give
- garden

It never changes sound.

Example

גבר

Gabar

to be strong / to prevail

Dalet —ד

Represents the sound D.

Example

דג

Dag

fish

Biblical Words

HEBREW	TRANSLITERATION	MEANING	STRONG
אב	Ab (av)	Father	H1
בן	Ban (ben)	Son	H1121
גבר	Gabar	To be strong	H1396
דג	Dag	Fish	H1709

EXERCISES — LESSON 1

0. Writing Practice

א ב ג ד

1. Letter Recognition

Identify the following letters:

א

ב

ג

ד

2. Reading the Letters

Read each letter aloud:

א — Alef

ב — Bet

ג— Gimel

ד — Dalet

3. Match Letter to Sound

Match each letter:

א → __

ב → __

ג → __

ד → __

(B, G, D, pause)

4. Word Breakdown

Separate the letters:

אב ______________________________

א ______________________________

ב ______________________________

בן ______________________________

ב ______________________________

ן ______________________________

דג ______________________________

ד ______________________________

ג ______________________________

5. Word Reconstruction

Complete the words:

אב → ב _

בן → _ ב

דג → ג _

6. Reading Practice

Read the words:

אב — Ab

בן— Ban

גבר— Gabar

דג — Dag

7. Comprehension

What do these words mean?

אב → ______

בן → ______

דג → ______

8. Letter Identification Inside Words

Identify the target letter:

Which letter is ג in this word?

גבר

Which letter is ד in this word?

דג

9. Oral Repetition

Read aloud several times:

אב

בן

דג

גבר

DAILY WALK WITH YAHUAH

A Guided Path — Lesson 1: Two Expressions to Know Yahuah

בקר טוב יהוה

Bakar Tob Yahuah

Good morning, Yahuah

אני בא אליך

Ani ba alakha

I come to You

Lesson Summary

In this lesson the student learned:

- four letters of the Hebrew alphabet
- how each letter sounds
- how to recognize each letter inside words
- four words from the Tanak

LESSON 2 — NEW LETTERS

Introduction

In this lesson we will continue learning new letters of the Hebrew alphabet. Each new letter will allow us to read more words from the Tanak.

Lesson Objective

The student will be able to:

• recognize the letters He, Waw, Zayin, and Het

• read words formed with these letters

Alphabet Letters

HEBREW	NAME	READING
ה	He	H (soft breathy sound)
ו	Waw	W / U
ז	Zayin	Z
ח	Het	strong guttural H

He — ה

He represents a soft breathy sound.

It is lighter than the strong guttural sound found in other letters, but it is not completely silent.

Biblical Example

היום

Course transliteration:

HaYom

Meaning:

The day

Note for the Student

In this course, the letter He (ה) is represented by the letter H in the transliteration.
When pronouncing it, the student should produce a soft breathy sound.

Biblical Words

HEBREW	TRANSLITERATION	MEANING	STRONG
דוד	Dawid	David	H1732
היה	Hayah	To be / to exist	H1961

Biblical Example

Text:

זה היום

Transliteration:

Zah HaYom

Meaning:

This is the day
(Psalm 118:24)

Note

In many academic materials this word is transliterated as Zeh, following the later Masoretic vocalization.
In this course, we use Zah as a simplified approximation within the pronunciation system of the course.

About the Letter ו — Waw

In this course we use the name Waw for the letter:

ו

In many modern materials this letter appears with the name Vav, but that form reflects a later pronunciation of Hebrew.

In older Hebrew, this letter likely had a sound closer to W, similar to the English w.

For that reason, throughout this course we will use:
Waw
as the name of the letter.

Approximate Sound

LETTER	NAME	APPROXIMATE SOUND
ו	Waw	w / u

Depending on the word, this letter may function as:

- a consonant W
- support for a vowel U / O

Biblical Example

והארץ
Course transliteration:
WaHaArats
Meaning:
And the earth
Here the letter ו (Waw) functions as the prefix:
Wa
and

Note for the Student

In this course, the name Waw will always be used instead of Vav when referring to this letter of the Hebrew alphabet.

EXERCISES — LESSON 2

0. Writing Practice

ה ו ז ח

1. Recognition of New Letters

Identify the following letters:

ה

ו

ז

ח

2. Review of Previous Letters

Read again the letters already learned:

א

ב

ג

ד

3. Combined Letter Review

Read all the letters learned so far:

א

ב

ג

ד

ה

ו

ז

ח

4. Breakdown of a Previous Word

Look at the word:

בן

Separate its letters:

ב

ן

5. Reconstruction of a Previous Word

Complete the word:

ב___

Answer:

בן

6. Breakdown of a New Word

Look at the word:

דוד

Separate its letters:

ד

ו

ד

7. Reconstruction of a New Word

Complete the word:

ד _ ד

Answer:

דוד

8. Reading a New Word

Read the word:

דוד

Expected transliteration:

Dawid

Meaning:

David

9. Reading a New Verb

Read the word:

היה

Expected transliteration:

Hayah

Meaning:

To be / to exist

10. Reading a Short Phrase

Read the phrase:

זה היום

Expected transliteration:

Zah HaYom

Meaning:

This is the day

11. Cumulative Review

Read aloud:

אב

בן

דוד

היה

12. Comprehension

What does the word mean?

דוד

Answer:

David

Daily Walk with Yahuah

A Guided Path — Lesson 2: Two Expressions to Know Yahuah

אתה אלהי

Atah Alohay

You are my Alohiym

אני עבדך

Ani abadakha

I am Your servant

Lesson Summary

The student now knows 8 letters of the Hebrew alphabet.

LESSON 3 — MORE LETTERS AND FIRST ROOTS

Introduction

Biblical Hebrew is built primarily around roots made of three consonants.
These roots carry the central idea behind many related words.
By learning to recognize Hebrew roots, students can begin to understand how many words in the Tanak are connected.

Lesson Objective

By the end of this lesson, the student will be able to:

- recognize new Hebrew letters
- understand the concept of a Hebrew root
- read additional words from the Tanak

New Letters

HEBREW	NAME	READING
ט	Tet	T
י	Yod	Y
כ	Kaf	K
ל	Lamed	L

Explanation of the Letters

Tet — ט

Represents the sound T.

It is always a strong T sound.

Example

טוב

Tob

good

Yod — י
Represents the sound Y (like “y” in yes).
Example
יד
Yad
hand

Kaf — כ
Represents the sound K.
Example
כל
Kol
all / everything

Lamed — ל
Represents the sound L.
Example
מלך
Malak
king

First Hebrew Root
Root:מלך
Consonants:
מ – ל – כ
Basic idea:
to reign / to rule
Many words related to kingship come from this root.

Biblical Words

HEBREW	TRANSLITERATION	MEANING	STRONG
מלך	Malak	King	H4428
יד	Yad	Hand	H3027
כל	Kol	All / everything	H3605
טוב	Tob	Good	H2896

Exercises — Lesson 3

0. Writing Practice

ט י כ ל

1. Recognition of New Letters

Identify the following letters:

ט

י

כ

ל

2. Reading the Letters

Read aloud:

ט — Tet

י — Yod

כ — Kaf

ל — Lamed

3. Match Letter to Sound

ט → ___

י → ___

כ → ___

ל → ___

(T, Y, K, L)

4. Word Breakdown

Separate the letters:

מלך

מ

ל

ך

טוב

ט

ו

ב

5. Word Reconstruction

Complete the words:

מ _ ך → מלך

ט _ ב → טוב

ד → יד _

6. Reading Practice

Read the words:

מלך— Malak

יד— Yad

כל — Kol

טוב — Tob

7. Identify the Letter Inside the Word

Where is ט in this word?

טוב

Where is ל in this word?

מלך

8. Cumulative Review (Lessons 1–3)

Read aloud:

אב

בן

דוד

היה

מלך

יד

כל

טוב

9. Cumulative Reconstruction

Complete:

אב → א _

בן → ב _

דוד → ד _ ד

מלך → מ _ ך

טוב → ט _ ב

10. Comprehension

What do the words mean?

מלך → ______________________________

יד → ______________________________

טוב → ______________________________

Daily Walk with Yahuah

A Guided Path — Lesson 3: Two Expressions to Know Yahuah

אני לפניך

Ani lafanakha

I am before You

שמע קולי

Shama qoli

Hear my voice

Lesson Summary

In this lesson the student learned:

- four new Hebrew letters
- the concept of a Hebrew root
- how roots connect words
- four new words from the Tanak

LESSON 4 — NEW LETTERS AND WORDS

Introduction

In this lesson we will continue learning additional letters of the Hebrew alphabet and new words from the Tanak.

Lesson Objective

The student will be able to:

• recognize new Hebrew letters
• read common words that appear in the Tanak

New Letters

HEBREW	NAME
מ	Mem
נ	Nun
ס	Samek
ע	Ayin

Explanation of the Letters

Mem —מ

Represents the sound M.

Example

מים

Mayim

water

Nun — נ

Represents the sound N.

Hebrew uses two forms of this letter:

• נ → regular form (beginning or middle)
• ן → final form (end of a word)

Examples

נתן

Natan

to give

בן

Ban (ben)

son

This word ends with Nun Sofit (ן)

Samek —**ס**

Represents the sound S.

Example

סוס

Sus

horse

Ayin —**ע**

Represents a deep guttural sound.

In this course it will often function as a vowel support.

Example

עם

Am

people / nation

Biblical Words

HEBREW	TRANSLITERATION	MEANING	STRONG
מים	Mayim	Water	H4325
עם	Am	People / nation	H5971
שם	Sham (Shem)	Name	H8034
סוס	Sus	Horse	H5483
נתן	Natan	To give	H5414
בן	Ban (ben)	Son	H1121

Biblical Example

עם ישראל

Transliteration:

Am Yasharal

Meaning:

The people of Israel

EXERCISES — LESSON 4

0. Writing Practice

מ נ ס ע

1. Recognition of New Letters

Identify the following letters:

מ

נ

ס

ע

2. Reading the Letters

Read aloud:

מ — Mem

נ — Nun

ס — Samek

ע — Ayin

3. Match Letter to Sound

מ → ___

נ → ___

ס → ___

ע → ___

(M, N, S, deep vowel)

4. Word Breakdown

Separate the letters:

מים

מ

י

ם

נתן

נ

ת

ן

בן

ב

ן

סוס

ס

ו

ס

5. Word Reconstruction

Complete the words:

מים → מ _ ם

נתן → נ _ ן

בן → ב _

סוס → ס _ ס

6. Reading Practice

Read the words:

מים — Mayim

עם — Am

שם — Sham

סוס — Sus

נתן — Natan

בן — Ban

7. Identify the Letter Inside the Word

Where is נ in this word?

נתן

Where is ן in this word?

בן

Where is ס in this word?

סוס

Where is ע in this word?

עם

8. Cumulative Review (Lessons 1–4)

Read aloud:

אב

בן

דוד

היה
מלך
יד
כל
מים
עם
שם
סוס
נתן

9. Cumulative Reconstruction

Complete the words:

א _ → אב
ב _ → בן
ד _ ד → דוד
מ _ ך → מלך
מ _ ם → מים
ס _ ס → סוס
נ _ ן → נתן

10. Comprehension

What do the words mean?

מים→ ______
עם → ______
נתן → ______

11. Oral Repetition

Read several times:

מים
עם
בן
סוס
נתן

Daily Walk with Yahuah

A Guided Path — Lesson 4: Two Expressions to Know Yahuah

אני קרא אליך

Ani qara alakha

I call to You

ענה לי

Anah li

Answer me

Lesson Summary

The student now:

- recognizes 4 new Hebrew letters
- understands the difference between Nun (נ) and Nun Sofit (ן)
- can identify each letter inside words
- continues building vocabulary from the Tanak

LESSON 5 — MORE LETTERS OF BIBLICAL HEBREW

Introduction

In this lesson we will continue learning additional letters of the Hebrew alphabet along with important words from the Tanak.

Lesson Objective

The student will be able to:

- recognize new Hebrew letters
- read frequently occurring biblical words

New Letters

HEBREW	NAME
פ	Pa (pe)
צ	Tsade
ק	Qof
ר	Resh

Explanation of the Letters

Pa (pe) — פ

Represents the sound P.

Example

פרי

Pari

fruit

Tsade — צ
Represents the sound TS (like in cats).
Example
צדיק
Tsadiq
righteous

Qof — ק
Represents a strong K sound (deeper than Kaf).
Example
קול
Qol
voice

Resh — ר
Represents the sound R.
Example
ארץ
Arats
earth / land

Biblical Words

HEBREW	TRANSLITERATION	MEANING	STRONG
ארץ	Arats	Earth / land	H776
צדיק	Tsadiq	Righteous	H6662
פרי	Pari	Fruit	H6529
קול	Qol	Voice	H6963

EXERCISES — LESSON 5

0. Writing Practice

פ צ ק ר

1. Recognition of New Letters

Identify:

פ

צ

ק

ר

2. Reading the Letters

Read aloud:

פ — Pa

צ — Tsade

ק — Qof

ר — Resh

3. Match Letter to Sound

פ → ___

צ → ___

ק → ___

ר → ___

(P, TS, K, R)

4. Word Breakdown

Separate:

ארץ

א

ר

ץ

קול

ק

ו
ל
פרי
פ
ר
י

5. Word Reconstruction

Complete:

א _ ץ → ארץ

פ _ י → פרי

ק _ ל → קול

6. Reading Practice

Read:

ארץ — Arats

צדיק — Tsadiq

פרי — Pari

קול — Qol

7. Identify the Letter Inside the Word

Where is ק in this word?

קול

Where is צ in this word?

צדיק

Where is פ in this word?

פרי

Where is ר in this word?

ארץ

8. Cumulative Review (Lessons 1–5)

Read aloud:

אב

בן

דוד

היה

מלך

יד

כל

מים

עם

שם

ארץ

צדיק

פרי

קול

9. Cumulative Reconstruction

Complete:

אב → א _

בן → ב _

מים → מ _ ם

ארץ → א _ ץ

פרי → פ _ י

קול → ק _ ל

10. Comprehension

What do the words mean?

ארץ → ______

פרי → ______

קול → ______

11. Oral Repetition

Read several times:

ארץ

צדיק

פרי

קול

Daily Walk with Yahuah

A Guided Path — Lesson 5: Two Expressions to Know Yahuah

אתה מלכי

Atah malki

You are my King

בך בטחתי

Bakha batahti

In You I have trusted

Lesson Summary

The student now:

- recognizes 4 new Hebrew letters
- can identify each letter inside words
- continues expanding vocabulary from the Tanak

LESSON 6 — FINAL LETTERS OF THE ALPHABET

Introduction

In this lesson we will learn the final letters of the Hebrew alphabet.

With these letters we will complete the Hebrew alphabet and begin reading our first short phrases from the Tanak.

Lesson Objective

By the end of this lesson the student will be able to:

- recognize the letters Shin and Taw
- identify all the letters of the Hebrew alphabet
- read a short biblical phrase

New Letters

HEBREW	NAME	READING
ש	Shin	Sh
ת	Taw	T

Explanation

Shin — ש

Represents the SH sound.

Example

שם

Sham (Shem)

name

Taw — ת

Represents the sound T.

Example

בת

Bat

daughter

Complete Alphabet Learned

אבגדהוזחטיכלמנסעפצקרשת

Biblical Words (Balanced)

HEBREW	TRANSLITERATION	MEANING	STRONG
שם	Sham (Shem)	Name	H8034
בת	Bat	Daughter	H1323
ברא	Bara	Created	H1254
אלהים	Alohiym	Alohiym	H430

First Biblical Reading

Text:

בראשית ברא אלהים

Transliteration:

Barashit Bara Alohiym

Meaning:

In the beginning Alohiym created

First Biblical Reading

Text:

בראשית ברא אלהים

Transliteration:

Barashit Bara Alohiym

Meaning:

In the beginning Alohiym created

EXERCISES — LESSON 6

0. Writing Practice

ש ת

1. Recognition of New Letters

Identify:

ש

ת

2. Reading the Letters

Read aloud:

ש — Shin

ת — Taw

3. Match Letter to Sound

ש→ ___

ת → ___

(SH, T)

4. Word Breakdown

Separate:

בת

ב

ת

ברא

ב

ר

א

5. Word Reconstruction

Complete:

בת → ב _

ברא → ב _ א

6. Reading Practice

Read:

שם — Sham

בת — Bat

ברא — Bara

7. Identify the Letter Inside the Word

Where is ת in this word?

בת

Where is ש in this word?

שם

8. Reading a Phrase

ברא אלהים

Transliteration:

Bara Alohiym

Meaning:

Alohiym created

9. Cumulative Review (Lessons 1–6)

Read aloud:

אב

בן

דוד

היה

מלך

יד
כל
מים
עם
שם
ארץ
צדיק
פרי
קול
נתן
בת
ברא
אלהים

10. Cumulative Reconstruction

Complete:

ב _ א → ברא
א _ ץ → ארץ
צ _ יק → צדיק
ב _ → בת
א _ → אב

11. Comprehension

What do the words mean?

בת → ______
ברא → ______

12. Oral Repetition

Read several times:

בת
שם
ברא
אלהים

Daily Walk with Yahuah

A Guided Path — Lesson 6: Two Expressions to Know Yahuah

עזרני יהוה

Azarani Yahuah

Help me, Yahuah

אל תעזבני

Al taazabani

Do not forsake me

Lesson Summary

The student now:

- recognizes the final two letters of the alphabet
- has completed the full Hebrew alphabet
- can identify and read all letters inside words
- can read a short biblical phrase

LESSON 7 — ROOTS OF BIBLICAL HEBREW

Introduction

Biblical Hebrew is built primarily from roots of three consonants.
These roots contain the central idea behind many related words.
Understanding roots allows the student to recognize many additional words in the Tanak.

Lesson Objective

The student will be able to:

- recognize Hebrew roots
- identify words related to the same root

Hebrew Root

מלך

Consonants:

M – L – K

Central idea:

to reign / to rule

Related Words

HEBREW	TRANSLITERATION	MEANING	STRONG
מלך	Malak	King	H4428
ממלכה	Mamlakah	Kingdom	H4467

Another Important Root

כתב

Central idea:

to write

Related Words

HEBREW	TRANSLITERATION	MEANING	STRONG
כתב	Katab	To write	H3789
כתבים	Katabiym	Writings	H3791

EXERCISES — LESSON 7

1. Reading New Roots

Read the following roots or words:

מלך

כתב

ממלכה

כתבים

2. Root Recognition

What is the root of the word?

מלך

Answer:

מלך

3. Root Recognition

What is the root of the word?

כתב

Answer:

כתב

4. Word Breakdown

Look at the word:

כתב

Separate its letters:

כ

ת

ב

5. Word Reconstruction

Complete the word:

כ _ ב

Answer:

כתב

6. Reading

כתב

Expected transliteration:

Katab

Meaning:

To write

7. Reading Related Words

מלך

Malak

King

ממלכה

Mamlakah

Kingdom

כתב

Katab

To write

כתבים

Katabiym

Writings

8. Cumulative Review (Lessons 1–7)

Read aloud:

אב

בן

דוד

היה

מלך

יד

כל

מים

עם

שם

ארץ

צדיק

פרי

ברא

אלהים

כתב

ממלכה

כתבים

9. Cumulative Reconstruction

Complete the words:

מ _ ך

כ _ ב

מ _ ם

א _ ץ

Answers:
מלך
כתב
מים
ארץ

10. Comprehension
What does the word mean?
כתב
Answer:
To write

11. Oral Repetition
Read several times:
מלך
כתב
ממלכה
כתבים

Daily Walk with Yahuah
A Guided Path — Lesson 7: Two Expressions to Know Yahuah
הדריכני בדרכך
Hadrikani badarakha
Guide me in Your way

הראני דרכך
Harani darakha
Show me Your way

Lesson Summary
In this lesson the student learned that:
- Biblical Hebrew uses three-consonant roots
- many words derive from the same root

LESSON 8 — PREFIXES IN BIBLICAL HEBREW

Introduction

Biblical Hebrew frequently uses prefixes to add meaning to words.
These prefixes appear constantly throughout the Tanak.

Lesson Objective

The student will be able to:

• recognize common prefixes
• understand how prefixes change the meaning of a word

Main Prefixes

HEBREW	TRANSLITERATION	MEANING
ו	Wa	And
ב	Ba	In
ל	La	to / for

Examples

HEBREW	TRANSLITERATION	MEANING
ומלך	WaMalak	and king
בארץ	BaArats	in the land
למלך	LaMalak	to the king

Example from the Tanak

ובראשית

Transliteration:

WaBarashit

Meaning:

And in the beginning

EXERCISES — LESSON 8

1. Prefix Recognition

Identify the following prefixes:

ו

ב

ל

2. Reading Prefixes

Read aloud:

ו = Wa

ב = Ba

ל = La

3. Word Breakdown with Prefix

Look at the word:

ומלך

Separate its parts:

ו

מלך

4. Word Reconstruction

Complete the word:

ו _ _ ך

Answer:

ומלך

5. Reading Words with Prefixes

ומלך

WaMalak

And king

בארץ
BaArats
In the land
למלך
LaMalak
To the king

6. Reading a Phrase
ובראשית
Expected transliteration:
WaBarashit
Meaning:
And in the beginning

7. Cumulative Review (Lessons 1–8)
Read aloud:
אב
בן
דוד
היה
מלך
יד
כל
מים
עם
שם
ארץ
צדיק
פרי
ברא
אלהים
כתב

ומלך
בארץ
למלך
ובראשית

8. Cumulative Reconstruction

Complete the words:

ו _ לך
ב _ רץ
ל _ לך

Answers:

ומלך
בארץ
למלך

9. Comprehension

What does the word mean?

ומלך

Answer:

And king

10. Oral Repetition

Read several times:

ומלך
בארץ
למלך

Daily Walk with Yahuah

A Guided Path — Lesson 8: Two Expressions to Know Yahuah

למדני אמתך

Lamadani amatakha

Teach me Your truth

פתח עיני

Patah aynay

Open my eyes

Lesson Summary

In this lesson the student learned that:

- Biblical Hebrew uses simple prefixes
- these prefixes appear frequently throughout the Tanak

LESSON 9 — THE DEFINITE ARTICLE

Introduction

Biblical Hebrew has a definite article equivalent to "the" in English. This article appears at the beginning of the word.

Lesson Objective

By the end of this lesson the student will be able to:

- recognize the definite article
- read words that include the article

The Definite Article

HEBREW	TRANSLITERATION	MEANING
ה	Ha	The

Examples

HEBREW	TRANSLITERATION	MEANING
הארץ	HaArats	the earth / the land
המלך	HaMalak	the king

New Word

HEBREW	TRANSLITERATION	MEANING	STRONG
איש	Ish	man	H376

Example

האיש

Transliteration:

HaIsh

Meaning:

the man

EXERCISES — LESSON 9

1. Article Recognition

Identify the letter used as the definite article:

ה

2. Reading Words with the Article

Read the following words:

הארץ

HaArats

The earth / the land

המלך

HaMalak

The king

האיש

HaIsh

The man

3. Word Breakdown with the Article

Look at the word:

הארץ

Separate its parts:

ה

ארץ

4. Word Reconstruction

Complete the word:

ה _ _ ץ

Answer:

הארץ

5. Reading a New Word

איש

Ish

Meaning:

man

6. Reading a Phrase

האיש

HaIsh

Meaning:

the man

7. Cumulative Review (Lessons 1–9)

Read aloud:

אב

בן

דוד

היה

מלך

יד

כל

מים

עם

שם

ארץ

צדיק

פרי

ברא

אלהים

כתב

ומלך

בארץ
למלך
הארץ
המלך
האיש

8. Cumulative Reconstruction

Complete the words:

ה _ רץ
ה _ לך
ה _ יש

Answers:

הארץ
המלך
האיש

9. Comprehension

What does the word mean?

הארץ

Answer:

the earth / the land

10. Oral Repetition

Read several times:

הארץ
המלך
האיש

Daily Walk with Yahuah

A Guided Path — Lesson 9: Two Expressions to Know Yahuah

בטחתי בך

Batahti bakha

I trust / have trusted in You

אתה מחסי

Atah mahsi

You are my refuge

Lesson Summary

The student learned:

- the definite article Ha
- how the article attaches to nouns

LESSON 10 — FINAL LETTERS (SOFIT)

Introduction

In Hebrew, some letters change their shape when they appear at the end of a word.

These forms are called Sofit (final forms).

Lesson Objective

By the end of this lesson the student will be able to:

• recognize final letters

• identify words that use them

Final Letters (Sofit)

NORMAL FORM	FINAL FORM	
כ	ך	Kaf
מ	ם	Mem
נ	ן	Nun
פ	ף	Pa
צ	ץ	Tsade

Examples

HEBREW	TRANSLITERATION	MEANING
מים	Mayim	water
מלך	Malak	king
בן	Ban	son
אלף	Alaf	thousand
ארץ	Arats	earth / land

EXERCISES — LESSON 10

0. Writing Practice

ך ם ן ף ץ

1. Recognition of Final Letters

Identify the following final letters:

ך

ם

ן

ף

ץ

2. Matching Normal and Final Forms

Match each letter with its final form:

כ → ך

מ → ם

נ → ן

פ → ף

צ → ץ

3. Identify the Final Letter in Words

Look at the words and identify the final letter:

מים

מלך

בן

אלף

ארץ

4. Word Breakdown

Separate the letters in each word:

מים

מ

י

ם

מלך

מ

ל

ך

בן

ב

ן

5. Word Reconstruction

Complete the words:

מ _ ם

מ _ ך

_ ב

א _ ף

א _ ץ

Answers:

מים

מלך

בן

אלף

ארץ

6. Reading Words with Final Letters

מים

Mayim
Water
מלך
Malak
King
בן
Ban (Ben)
Son
אלף
Alaf
Thousand
ארץ
Arats
Earth / land

7. Cumulative Review (Lessons 1–10)
Read aloud:
אב
בן
דוד
היה
מלך
יד
כל
מים
עם
שם
ארץ
צדיק
פרי
ברא

אלהים
כתב
ומלך
בארץ
למלך
הארץ
המלך
האיש
אלף

8. Comprehension

Which final letter appears in the word:

מים

Answer:

ם

Which final letter appears in the word:

מלך

Answer:

ך

9. Oral Repetition

Read several times:

מים
מלך
בן
אלף
ארץ

Daily Walk with Yahuah

A Guided Path — Lesson 10: Two Expressions to Know Yahuah

אתה עמי

Atah ami

You are with me

אני לא אירא

Ani la ira

I will not fear

Lesson Summary

The student learned:

- the five final letters (Sofit)
- that these forms appear only at the end of a word

End of Level 1

YADA YAHUAH

BIBLICAL HEBREW

Learn to Read the Hebrew of the Scriptures
and Discover the Name Yahuah.

— ידע יהוה —

Level 2

FOUNDATIONS OF BIBLICAL HEBREW

After completing Level 1 of this course, the student has learned the essential foundations needed to begin reading Biblical Hebrew.
In these first lessons the student studied:
- the 22 letters of the Hebrew alphabet
- the final forms (Sofit)
- fundamental words from the Tanak
- basic Hebrew roots
- the first elements of reading

Thanks to this knowledge, the student can now recognize the letters of Biblical Hebrew and read words that appear in the text of the Scriptures.
This is an important step in the process of learning the language.
The next level of the course introduces new elements that will help the student better understand how words function within the sentences of the Tanak.

Level 2

Structure of Biblical Hebrew
In Level 2, the student will begin studying several important elements that appear constantly throughout the text of the Scriptures.

These include:
- prefixes in Biblical Hebrew
- the definite article
- plural forms
- the construct state
- personal pronouns
- fundamental verbs
- the order of phrases in Hebrew

These elements will make it easier to recognize many grammatical structures that appear in the Tanak.
As the student progresses through these lessons, they will begin reading complete phrases and better understand how expressions are constructed in Biblical Hebrew.

This level prepares the student for the next step of the course:
direct reading of the Tanak.

In this way, the study of the language continues bringing the student closer to the purpose expressed in the name of this course:
ידע יהוה
Yada Yahuah
To know Yahuah.

YADA YAHUAH

BIBLICAL HEBREW

Learn to Read the Hebrew of the Scriptures and Discover the Name Yahuah.

— ידע יהוה —

Level 2

INTRODUCTION

In Level 1 of this course, the student learned the essential foundations needed to begin recognizing Biblical Hebrew.
Throughout the first lessons, the student studied the letters of the Hebrew alphabet, the final letter forms (Sofit), and several words that frequently appear in the text of the Tanak.

After completing that level, the student is now able to:
- identify the letters of the Hebrew alphabet
- read basic Hebrew words
- recognize simple structures that appear in the Scriptures

In Level 2, we will begin studying how Biblical Hebrew functions inside phrases and sentences found in the text of the Scriptures.
In these lessons the student will learn several important elements that appear constantly in the Tanak, including:
- Hebrew roots
- common prefixes
- the definite article
- plural forms
- the construct state
- pronouns
- fundamental verbs
- the word order of Biblical Hebrew sentences

These elements will help the student understand how expressions and phrases are formed within the language.
As the student progresses through these lessons, they will begin to recognize many words and grammatical structures that appear throughout the Hebrew text of the Scriptures.

The goal of this level is to prepare the student for the next step:
reading phrases and verses from the Tanak directly in Hebrew.
In this way, the study of the language continues advancing toward the purpose expressed in the name of this course:
ידע יהוה
Yada Yahuah
To know Yahuah.

LESSON 11 — REVIEW OF LESSONS 1–10

Introduction

In the first ten lessons we learned the foundations of Biblical Hebrew:

- the 22 letters of the Hebrew alphabet
- basic words from the Tanak
- the Hebrew root system
- common prefixes
- the definite article
- the final letters (Sofit)

In this lesson we will review these elements to strengthen reading ability before continuing with new structures of the language.

Lesson Objective

By the end of this lesson the student will be able to:

- recognize all the letters of the Hebrew alphabet
- read basic words from the Tanak
- identify prefixes and articles
- recognize final letters

Alphabet Review

א ב ג ד ה ו ז ח ט י כ ל מ נ ס ע פ צ ק ר ש ת

Words Learned (Expanded Review)

HEBREW	TRANSLITERATION	MEANING
אב	Ab	Father
בן	Ban	Son
דוד	Dawid	David
היה	Hayah	To be
מלך	Malak	King
יד	Yad	Hand
כל	Kol	All
מים	Mayim	Water
עם	Am	People
שם	Sham	Name
ארץ	Arats	Earth
צדיק	Tsadiq	Righteous
פרי	Pari	Fruit
קול	Qol	Voice
נתן	Natan	To give
בת	Bat	Daughter
ברא	Bara	Created
אלהים	Alohiym	God / gods

EXERCISES — LESSON 11

1. Letter Recognition

Identify:

א

מ

ר

ש

ת

נ

2. Full Alphabet Review

Read aloud:

א ב ג ד ה ו ז ח ט י כ ל מ נ ס ע פ צ ק ר ש ת

3. Reading Practice

Read the words:

אב

בן

דוד

מלך

מים

ארץ

שם

יד

פרי

קול

נתן

בת

4. Word Breakdown

Separate:

מלך

מ

ל

ך

נתן

נ

ת

ן

ארץ

א

ר

ץ

5. Word Reconstruction

Complete:

מ _ ך → מלך

מ _ ם → מים

א _ ץ → ארץ

נ _ ן → נתן

ב _ → בת

6. Prefix Recognition

Look at the words:

ומלך → _____

בארץ → _____

למלך → _____

Answers:

ו = and

ב = in

ל = to / for

7. Article Recognition

Look at the words:

הארץ → _____

המלך → _____

האיש → _____

Answer:

ה = the

8. Final Letters (Sofit Recognition)

Identify the final letters:

מים → ם

מלך → ך

בן → ן

ארץ → ץ

9. Cumulative Reading (Strong)

Read aloud:

אב

בן

דוד

היה

מלך

יד

כל

מים

עם

שם

ארץ

צדיק

פרי

קול

נתן
בת
ברא
אלהים

10. Mixed Reading

Read:

ומלך
בארץ
למלך
ברא אלהים

11. Comprehension

What do the words mean?

מלך → _____
מים → _____
נתן → _____
→ בת _____

12. Oral Repetition

Read several times:

מלך
מים
ארץ
נתן
ברא

Daily Walk with Yahuah

A Guided Path — Lesson 11: Two Expressions to Know Yahuah

אני חלש

Ani halash

I am weak

חזקני

Hazakani

Strengthen me

Lesson Summary

This lesson reviewed:

- the complete Hebrew alphabet
- key vocabulary from Lessons 1–10
- prefixes and the article
- final letter forms (Sofit)
- reading fluency using real biblical words

LESSON 12 — THE PLURAL IN BIBLICAL HEBREW

Introduction

Biblical Hebrew has specific forms used to express more than one.
One of the most common plural endings is:

ים

Transliteration used in this course:
-iym

Lesson Objective

By the end of this lesson the student will be able to:

- recognize the masculine plural form
- form simple plural words
- identify common plural patterns

How to Form the Plural

Basic idea:
Add -iym (**ים**) to the word.

Step-by-Step Example

Singular:
מלך
Malak
king
Add ending:
מלך + ים
Result:
מלכים
Malakiym
kings

Examples

SINGULAR	PLURAL	MEANING
יום (Yom)	ימים (Yamiym)	day → days
מלך (Malak)	מלכים (Malakiym)	king → kings
בן (Ban)	בנים (Baniym)	son → sons

Important Observation

The word may change slightly when forming the plural.
This is normal in Hebrew.

Additional Examples

SINGULAR	PLURAL	MEANING
דבר (Dabar)	דברים (Dabariym)	word → words
עם (Am)	עמים (Amiym)	people → peoples

Special Cases

Some words:
look plural
but do not behave like regular plurals

מים

Mayim
water
✓ has plural form
✓ used as a singular concept
✓ does not form another plural

שמים

Shamayim
heavens

✓ always appears in plural form

פנים

Paniym

face

✓ plural form

✓ often used as singular

אלהים

Alohiym

✓ plural form

✓ may be singular or plural depending on context

EXERCISES — LESSON 12

1. Form the Plural

Write the plural:

מלך → ______

בן → ______

יום → ______

2. Word Breakdown

ימים

Separate the letters:

י

מ

י

ם

3. Word Reconstruction

Complete:

מ _ כ י ם → מלכים

ב _ י ם → בנים

4. Reading Practice

Read:

מלכים — Malakiym

בנים — Baniym

ימים — Yamiym

5. Identify the Ending

What is the plural ending in:

מלכים → _____

בנים → _____

Answer:

ים (-iym)

6. Singular vs Plural

Match:

מלך → _____

מלכים → _____

בן → _____

בנים → _____

7. Cumulative Reading

Read aloud:

בן

בנים

מלך

מלכים

יום

ימים

עם

עמים

8. Special Case Recognition

Which words look plural?

מים

שמים

פנים

אלהים

9. Comprehension

What do the words mean?

בנים → _____

מלכים → _____

Daily Walk with Yahuah

A Guided Path — Lesson 12: Two Expressions to Know Yahuah

אני בצרה

Ani batsarah

I am in distress

נחמני

Nahamani

Comfort me

Lesson Summary

The student learned:

- the masculine plural ending -iym (**ים**)
- how to form plural words
- that some words change slightly
- that some words have plural form but special meaning

LESSON 13 — THE CONSTRUCT STATE

Introduction

Biblical Hebrew uses a special structure to connect two words.
This structure is called the construct state.
It expresses a relationship similar to "of" in English.

Lesson Objective

By the end of this lesson the student will be able to:

• recognize the construct state
• understand how to express "of" in Hebrew
• build simple construct phrases

How Hebrew Expresses "Of"

In English:
"king of Israel"
In Hebrew:
מלך ישראל
There is NO word for "of"

Rule
Hebrew places two words together:
Word 1 + Word 2

Structure

POSITION	FUNCTION
First word	thing described
Second word	owner / description

Step-by-Step Example

English:

King of Israel

Step 1 — Identify words

King → מלך

Yasharal → ישראל

Step 2 — Remove "of"

Step 3 — Combine

מלך ישראל

Malak Yasharal

King of Israel

Examples

HEBREW	TRANSLITERATION	MEANING
מלך ישראל	Malak Yasharal	King of Israel
בן האיש	Ban HaIsh	Son of the man
שם המלך	Sham HaMalak	Name of the king

Important Note

Hebrew does not write "of"

The connection is shown by:

- word order
- direct placement

How to Build It Yourself

Example:

מלך (king)

הארץ (the land)

Combine:

מלך הארץ

King of the land

EXERCISES — LESSON 13

1. Reading a Construct Phrase

מלך ישראל

2. Comprehension

What does it mean?

מלך ישראל → _____

3. Identify the Order

בן האיש

First word: _____

Second word: _____

4. Build the Phrase

Write in Hebrew:

King of the land

Words:

מלך

הארץ

Answer:

---

5. Build Another Phrase

Son of the king

Words:

בן

המלך

Answer:

---

6. Word Separation

Separate:

מלך ישראל

→ ______

→ ______

7. Phrase Reconstruction

Complete:

מ _ ך י _ ר _ ל

Answer:

מלך ישראל

8. Additional Reading

שם המלך

Sham HaMalak

Name of the king

9. Cumulative Reading

Read aloud:

מלך ישראל

בן האיש

שם המלך

מלך הארץ

10. Mini Transformation Exercise

Change to Hebrew:

"son of the man"

Words:

בן

האיש

Answer:

Note

In Biblical Hebrew, another word for “man” is:

אדם (Adam)

You will learn this word in a later lesson.

Daily Walk with Yahuah

A Guided Path — Lesson 13: Two Expressions to Know Yahuah

שמע תחנתי

Shama tahanati

Hear my supplication

רחם עלי

Raham alay

Have mercy on me

Lesson Summary

The student learned:

- Hebrew does not use a word for “of”
- “of” is expressed by placing two words together
- how to build simple construct phrases
- how word order creates meaning

LESSON 14 — PERSONAL PRONOUNS

Introduction

Pronouns indicate who performs the action in a sentence.
Personal pronouns appear frequently in Biblical Hebrew, especially when identifying the subject of a statement.

Lesson Objective

By the end of this lesson the student will be able to:
• recognize basic personal pronouns in Biblical Hebrew

Pronouns (Personal Pronouns)

Biblical Hebrew distinguishes between:
• singular and plural
• masculine and feminine

Singular Pronouns

HEBREW	TRANSLITERATION	MEANING
אני	Ani	I
אתה	Atah	You (masculine singular)
את	At	You (feminine singular)
הוא	Hu	He
היא	Hi	She

Plural Pronouns

HEBREW	TRANSLITERATION	MEANING
אנחנו	Anachnu	We
אתם	Atam (atem)	You (masculine plural)
אתן	Atan (aten)	You (feminine plural)
הם	Ham (hem)	They (masculine)
הן	Han (hen)	They (feminine)

Important Notes for the Student

- Hebrew distinguishes between masculine and feminine forms.
- Hebrew also distinguishes between singular and plural "you".
- In English, "you" can refer to one person or many people, but in Hebrew these forms are different.

Simple Examples

אני

Ani

I

אתה מלך

Atah Malak

You (masc.) are a king

הם מלכים

Ham Malakiym

They are kings

EXERCISES — LESSON 14

1. Reading Pronouns

אני

Ani

I

2. Reading

הוא

Hu

He

3. Additional Reading

אתה

Atah

You

4. Word Breakdown

אני

Separate the letters:

א

נ

י

5. Word Reconstruction

Complete:

א _ י

Answer:

אני

6. Cumulative Review

Read aloud:

אני

אתה

הוא

היא

7. Comprehension

What does this word mean?

הוא

Answer:

He

Daily Walk with Yahuah

A Guided Path — Lesson 14: Two Expressions to Know Yahuah

חטאתי לך

Hatati lakha

I have sinned against You

סלח לי

Salah li

Forgive me

Lesson Summary

The student learned basic personal pronouns in Biblical Hebrew.

LESSON 15 — POSSESSIVE PRONOUNS

Introduction

In Biblical Hebrew, possession is often expressed by adding a suffix to the end of a word.
These suffixes indicate relationships such as:
my, your, his, her, our, your (plural), their

Lesson Objective

The student will be able to:

- recognize possessive suffixes
- understand how they attach to words
- read basic possessive forms in the Tanak

Base Example

HEBREW	TRANSLITERATION	MEANING
אב	Ab	father

Possessive Forms (Model Word: אב)

HEBREW	TRANSLITERATION	MEANING
אבי	Abi	my father
אביך	Abikha	your father (masculine singular)
אביו	Abiyu	his father
אביה	Abiha	her father
אבינו	Abinu	our father
אביכם	Abikham	your father (plural masculine)
אביכן	Abikhan	your father (plural feminine)
אביהם	Abiham	their father (masculine)
אביהן	Abihan	their father (feminine)

What to Observe

The base word remains visible:

אב → אבי

אב → אביו

The meaning changes through the suffix

The word itself is not replaced

Applying the Same Pattern to Other Words

The same suffixes can be attached to many Hebrew words.

Example 1 — מלך (Malak — king)

HEBREW	TRANSLITERATION	MEANING
מלכי	Malki	my king
מלכך	Malkha	your king
מלכו	Malko	his king
מלכה	Malkah	her king
מלכנו	Malkanu	our king
מלכיהם	Malkiham	their king

Example 2 — ארץ (Arats — land)

HEBREW	TRANSLITERATION	MEANING
ארצי	Artsi	my land
ארצך	Artskha	your land
ארצו	Artso	his land
ארצה	Artsah	her land
ארצנו	Artsanu	our land
ארצם	Artsam	their land

Example 3 — שם (Sham "shem"— name)

HEBREW	TRANSLITERATION	MEANING
שמי	Shami	my name
שמך	Shamkha	your name
שמו	Shamo	his name
שמה	Shamah	her name
שמנו	Shamanu	our name
שמם	Shamam	their name

Important Observations

- The suffix attaches directly to the word
- The word may change slightly in pronunciation
- The root remains recognizable

Key Learning Insight

Hebrew does not use separate words like "my" or "your"
Instead, it attaches the meaning to the word itself

Simplified Learning Tip

Focus first on recognizing these common suffixes:

HEBREW	TRANSLITERATION	MEANING
שמי	Shami	my name
שמך	Shamkha	your name
שמו	Shamo	his name
שמה	Shamah	her name
שמנו	Shamanu	our name
שמם	Shamam	their name

Practice

Read the following:

מלכי

Malki

my king

ארצנו

Artsanu

our land

שמו

Shamo

his name

אביהם

Abiham

their father

EXERCISES — LESSON 15

1. Reading Possessive Forms

Read the following:

אבי

Abi

My father

אביו

Abiyu

His father

אבינו
Abinu
Our father

2. Comparison
Observe the difference:
אב
Ab
Father

אבי
Abi
My father

אביו
Abiyu
His father
What changed?
Write your answer:

(Hint: Look at the ending of the word. What was added?)

3. Word Breakdown
Separate the letters:
אבי
א
ב
י

4. Word Reconstruction

Complete the word:

א _ י

Answer:

אבי

5. Recognizing Suffixes

Identify the meaning of the suffix:

אבי

Suffix: ______

Meaning: ______

אביו

Suffix: ______

Meaning: ______

אבינו

Suffix: ______

Meaning: ______

6. Applying the Pattern

Complete the meaning:

מלכי

________ king

שמו

his ______

ארצנו

our ______

7. Mini Sentence Reading

Read the sentence:

מלכי טוב

Transliteration:

Malki Tob (tov)

Meaning:

My king is good

What to observe:

- **מלכי** = my king
- **טוב** = good

This shows how possessive forms appear inside simple Hebrew phrases.

8. Cumulative Reading

Read aloud:

אב

אבי

אביו

אבינו

בן

בנים

9. Comprehension

What does the word mean?

אביו

Answer:

Important Example — Yahuah Alohiym

In Biblical Hebrew, possessive suffixes are added to nouns, not to proper names.

For this reason, the Name:

יהוה

Yahuah

does not take possessive endings.

Correct Usage

To express possession, the suffix is added to **אלהים** (Alohiym), not to**יהוה** .

Examples

HEBREW	TRANSLITERATION	MEANING
יהוה אלהי	Yahuah Alohay	Yahuah my Alohiym
יהוה אלהינו	Yahuah Alohaynu	Yahuah our Alohiym

What to Observe

- **יהוה** (Yahuah) does not change
- The suffix is added to **אלהים** (Alohiym)
- The meaning changes through the suffix

Important Rule

❌ Do not say:
- Yahuahi
- Yahuahnu

✓ Instead say:
- Yahuah Alohay (my Elohiym)
- Yahuah Alohaynu (our Elohiym)

Key Insight

Hebrew attaches possession to the noun, not to the proper name

10. Application — Yahuah Alohiym

Complete the phrases:

יהוה אלהי

Transliteration: ________________

Meaning: ________________

יהוה אלהינו

Transliteration: _______________

Meaning: _______________

11. Reflection

What changed in these phrases?

(Hint: Which word received the suffix?)

Daily Walk with Yahuah

A Guided Path — Lesson 15: Two Expressions to Know Yahuah

טהר לבי

Tahar libi

Cleanse my heart

חדש רוחי

Hadash ruhi

Renew my spirit

Lesson Summary

The student learned:

- that possessive meaning can be added at the end of a word
- that suffixes indicate relationships such as my, his, our
- how to recognize these suffixes in words
- how possessive forms appear inside simple Hebrew phrases

LESSON 16 — A FUNDAMENTAL VERB OF BIBLICAL HEBREW

Introduction

Verbs are essential for understanding actions within the biblical text.
In this lesson we will study one of the most important verbs in Biblical Hebrew:
היה (Hayah)

Lesson Objective

By the end of this lesson the student will be able to:

- recognize the verb Hayah
- understand how verbs appear in the Tanak
- identify the verb in different forms

HEBREW	TRANSLITERATION	MEANING	STRONG
היה	Hayah	To be / to exist	H1961

Important Observation

In Biblical Hebrew, verbs do not always appear in one fixed form
The same root can appear differently in the text

Biblical Example

והיה
WaHayah
and it was / and it shall be

Important Note

Biblical Hebrew often does not use a verb for "am / is / are" in simple sentences
Example:
אני מלך

Ani Malak
I am king
(No verb to be is written)

Important Biblical Expression
אהיה אשר אהיה
Ahyah Asher Ahyah
I am that I am

Explanation
This expression comes from the root:
היה (Hayah)
But here it appears as:
אהיה (Ahyah)
This shows:
✓ the same root
✓ in a different form
✓ with the idea of existence

Do not try to memorize forms
Instead:
• recognize the root
• recognize the meaning
• understand the context

Examples in Context
הוא היה
Hu Hayah
He was

והיה
WaHayah
And it was / and it shall be

EXERCISES — LESSON 16

1. Reading the Verb

היה

Hayah

2. Reading with Prefix

והיה

WaHayah

3. Word Breakdown

היה

ה

י

ה

4. Word Reconstruction

Complete:

ה _ ה

Answer:

היה

5. Recognition

Which word comes from the root **היה**?

אהיה

מלך

בן

Answer:

אהיה

6. Reading Expressions

Read:

והיה

אהיה אשר אהיה

7. Cumulative Review

Read aloud:

היה

והיה

ברא

אמר

8. Comprehension

What does the root mean?

היה → _____

Daily Walk with Yahuah

A Guided Path — Lesson 16: Two Expressions to Know Yahuah

אני חפץ לדעת יהוה

Ani hafats ladaat Yahuah

I desire to know Yahuah

קרבני אליך

Qarabani alakha

Bring me near to You

Lesson Summary

The student learned:

- the root **היה** (Hayah)
- that verbs appear in different forms in the Tanak
- that Hebrew does not always use "to be" in the present
- how to recognize the verb in context

LESSON 17 — WORD ORDER IN BIBLICAL HEBREW

Introduction

Biblical Hebrew often uses a different word order than English.

A very common structure is:
Verb → Subject → Object

However:
This is not the only structure used in Hebrew.

Lesson Objective

The student will be able to:

- recognize common Hebrew word order
- understand how meaning is formed in a sentence
- rearrange Hebrew phrases into English
- recognize that word order can change for emphasis

Biblical Example

Text:
ברא אלהים
Transliteration:
Bara Alohiym
Meaning:
Alohiym created

Explanation

PART	MEANING
ברא	created (verb)
אלהים	Alohiym (subject)

The verb appears first, followed by the subject

Key Principle

Biblical Hebrew often begins with the action (verb)

English usually begins with the subject

Important Nuance

Hebrew does NOT always follow one fixed order

Two common patterns:

1. Verb → Subject

Action-focused

ברא אלהים

Bara Alohiym

Alohiym created

2. Subject → Verb

Subject-focused

יהוה יברכך

Yahuah Yabarakha

Yahuah will bless you

What Changes?

The emphasis

ORDER	FOCUS
Verb first	Action
Subject first	subject

How to Work with Hebrew Word Order

Step 1 — Find the verb
What is happening?

Step 2 — Find the subject
Who is doing it?
Step 3 — Rearrange for English
Put subject first

Additional Examples

HEBREW	TRANSLITERATION	MEANING
אמר משה	Amar Moshe	Moshe said
שמע ישראל	Shama Yasharal	Israel heard / Hear O Israel
יהוה יברכך	Yahuah Yabarakha	Yahuah will bless you

EXERCISES — LESSON 17

1. Reading the Phrase
ברא אלהים

2. Identify the Parts
→ ברא ______
→ אלהים ______

3. Rearranging Exercise
Reorder into English:
ברא אלהים
Answer:

4. Guided Practice
Text:

אמר משה
Step 1 — Verb: _____
Step 2 — Subject: _____
Step 3 — English: _____ _____

5. Compare the Order
Look at both:
ברא אלהים
יהוה יברכך
Which one starts with the verb?
Which one starts with the subject?

6. Build the Meaning
Translate:
שמע ישראל
Answer:

7. Build Hebrew Order
Translate into Hebrew order:
"Alohiym created"
Words:
אלהים
ברא
Answer:

8. Reverse Thinking
Given:
Yahuah will bless you
Write in Hebrew order:

9. Cumulative Reading

Read aloud:

ברא אלהים

אמר משה

שמע ישראל

יהוה יברכך

10. Comprehension

What does this mean?

אמר משה

Answer:

Daily Walk with Yahuah

A Guided Path — Lesson 17: Two Expressions to Know Yahuah

הראני ארחך

Harani orhakha

Show me Your path

שמרני בדרכך

Shamarani badarakha

Keep me in Your way

Lesson Summary

The student learned:

- the common Hebrew word order (Verb → Subject)
- that Hebrew word order is flexible
- that word order can change emphasis
- how to identify and rearrange Hebrew sentences

LESSON 18 — READING THE FIRST VERSES OF THE TANAK

Introduction

In this lesson we will read one of the most well-known verses in the Scriptures:
Genesis 1:1
And we will begin to read the next part of the text.

Lesson Objective

The student will be able to:

- read a complete verse from the Tanak
- recognize known words in context
- begin reading beyond a single verse
- apply previously learned structures

First Verse

Hebrew Text

בראשית ברא אלהים את השמים ואת הארץ

Course Transliteration

Barashit Bara Alohiym at HaShamayim WaAt HaArats

Meaning

In the beginning Alohiym created the heavens and the earth.

Word Breakdown

HEBREW	TRANSLITERATION	MEANING
בראשית	Barashit	In the beginning
ברא	Bara	Created
אלהים	Alohiym	Alohiym
השמים	HaShamayim	The heavens
הארץ	HaArats	The earth

New Reading

Hebrew Text

והארץ היתה תהו ובהו

Transliteration

WaHaArats Hayatah Tohu WaBohu

Meaning

And the earth was formless and empty

New Words

HEBREW	TRANSLITERATION	MEANING
היתה	Hayatah	was
תהו	Tohu	formless
ובהו	WaBohu	and empty

What the Student Should Notice

והארץ (WaHaArats)

✓ prefix ו (and)

✓ article ה (the)

היתה (Hayatah)

✓ comes from the root היה (Hayah)

Word order still follows Hebrew patterns

EXERCISES — LESSON 18

1. Reading (Verse 1)

בראשית ברא אלהים

2. Reading

והארץ היתה תהו ובהו

3. Word Breakdown

בראשית

ב

ר

א

ש

י

ת

4. Word Reconstruction

Complete:

_ ב _ א _ י

Answer:

בראשית

5. Identify Known Elements

In the word:

והארץ

Identify:

Prefix: ______

Article: ______

6. Recognition

Which word comes from the root **היה**?

היתה

ארץ

שמים

Answer: ______

7. Cumulative Reading

Read aloud:

בראשית

ברא

אלהים

והארץ

היתה

8. Comprehension

What does this mean?

והארץ היתה

Answer:

9. Mini Analysis Exercise

Break the phrase:

והארץ היתה

→ ______ (and the earth)

→ ______ (was)

10. Full Reading Practice

Read slowly:

בראשית ברא אלהים את השמים ואת הארץ

והארץ היתה תהו ובהו

Daily Walk with Yahuah

A Guided Path — Lesson 18: Two Expressions to Know Yahuah

דברך אמת

Dabarakha amat

Your word is truth

למדני דברך

Lamadani dabarakha

Teach me Your word

Lesson Summary

The student:

- read Genesis 1:1 completely
- began reading the next verse
- recognized known words in a new context
- identified prefixes and verb forms
- expanded beyond a single verse

LESSON 19 — MASTERING FREQUENT WORDS OF THE TANAK

Introduction

Some words appear thousands of times in the Tanak.
Learning these words allows the student to:
recognize large portions of the text
understand phrases more quickly
read with greater confidence

Lesson Objective

The student will be able to:

- recognize high-frequency words
- understand their function in sentences
- combine them into meaningful phrases
- identify them in biblical context

Core High-Frequency Words

1. Particles (Structure Words)

HEBREW	TRANSLITERATION	MEANING
ו	Wa	and
את	At	direct object marker
ב	Ba	in
ל	La	to / for
ה	Ha	the

2. Core Nouns

HEBREW	TRANSLITERATION	MEANING
אלהים	Alohiym	God / gods
יהוה	Yahuah	Name of the Creator
בן	Ban	Son
ארץ	Arats	Earth
יום	Yom	Day
מים	Mayim	Water
מלך	Malak	King

How These Words Work Together

Example 1

והארץ

Wa + Ha + Arats

and + the + earth

Example 2

את הארץ

At HaArats

(marker) the earth

Example 3

בן המלך

Ban HaMalak

son of the king

Key Insight

These small words:

- connect meaning
- define relationships
- structure sentences

Without them, reading is incomplete

Pattern Recognition

Prefixes

PREFIX	MEANING	EXAMPLE
ו	and	והארץ
ב	in	בארץ
ל	to	למלך

Article

Prefix Meaning

ה The

Example:

הארץ→ the earth

EXERCISES — LESSON 19

1. Identify the Parts

והארץ

Prefix: _____

Article: _____

Word: _____

2. Build the Meaning

Translate:

בארץ

→ _____

3. Combine Words

Form the phrase:

"son of the king"

Words:

בן
המלך
Answer:

4. Recognize the Function

What is the role of:
את
Answer:

5. Reading Practice

Read:
והארץ
בארץ
למלך
את הארץ

6. Phrase Analysis

בן הארץ
→ ______ of the earth

7. Build a Phrase

Translate into Hebrew:
"and the king"
Words:
ו
המלך
Answer:

8. Reverse Thinking

Given:
והארץ

Break it into parts:

→ ______

→ ______

→ ______

9. Cumulative Reading

Read aloud:

בן

המלך

והארץ

בארץ

למלך

את הארץ

10. Mini Reading

Read and understand:

והמלך בארץ

Answer:

Mini Context Reading

Read:

והמלך בארץ

Transliteration:

WaHaMalak BaArats

Meaning:

And the king is in the land

Daily Walk with Yahuah

A Guided Path — Lesson 19: Two Expressions to Know Yahuah

ברכני יהוה

Barakani Yahuah

Bless me, Yahuah

שמרני מכל רע

Shamarani mikol ra

Keep me from all evil

Lesson Summary

The student learned:

- high-frequency words of the Tanak
- how prefixes and particles function
- how to combine words into phrases
- how to analyze and build meaning

LESSON 20 — FUNDAMENTAL ROOTS AND FIRST VERB FORMS

Introduction

Many Biblical Hebrew words come from three-consonant roots.
Learning these roots allows the student to recognize many words in the Tanak.
In this lesson, we will also begin to see how these roots are used to express who is performing the action.

Lesson Objective

The student will be able to:

- recognize important Hebrew roots
- understand basic verb meaning
- identify simple verb forms
- recognize who performs the action

Frequent Roots

HEBREW	TRANSLITERATION	MEANING	STRONG
ברא	Bara	create	H1254
אמר	Amar	say	H559
עשה	Asah	do / make	H6213
נתן	Natan	give	H5414
הלך	Halak	walk	H1980
ראה	Raah	see	H7200
שמע	Shama	hear	H8085
ידע	Yada	know	H3045
שמר	Shamar	guard	H8104
ברך	Barak	bless	H1288

First Verb Forms

Hebrew verbs change slightly to show who is doing the action.
We will learn four basic forms:

MEANING	HEBREW (ברך)	TRANSLITERATION
I (blessed)	ברכתי	Barakti
You (blessed, m)	ברכת	Barakta
He (blessed)	ברך	Barak
She (blessed)	ברכה	Barakah

Important Observation

The root stays the same:

ב ר ך

But the ending changes.

Pattern to Notice

HEBREW	NAME
פ	Pa (pe)
צ	Tsade
ק	Qof
ר	Resh

Example with Another Root

שמע (Shama — hear)

ENDING	MEANING
-תי	I
-ת	You
(no ending)	He
-ה	She

Example with Another Root

ידע — Yada (to know)

MEANING	HEBREW (ברך)	TRANSLITERATION
I (blessed)	ברכתי	Barakti
You (blessed, m)	ברכת	Barakta
He (blessed)	ברך	Barak
She (blessed)	ברכה	Barakah

Correct Biblical Expression

ידעתי את יהוה

Yada'ti at Yahuah

"I have known Yahuah" / "I came to know Yahuah"

Course Teaching Note

In this course:

✓ the root form is used to express the general idea of the action

✓ the -ti form is used to express a completed action

Example Expressions

Expression Meaning

אני ידע יהוה Ani Yada Yahuah - I know Yahuah (course simplified form)

ידעתי את יהוה Yadaʿti at Yahuah - I knew / I have known Yahuah

Key Teaching Line

The form expresses the action.

The exact time (past or present) often depends on context in Biblical Hebrew.

Another Example

שמע ישראל

Shama Yasharal

"Hear, O Yasharal"

✓ same root

✓ same base form

✓ used here as a command

What the Student Should Understand

The root gives the meaning.

The ending shows the subject.

EXERCISES — LESSON 20

1. Reading Roots

שמע — Shama — hear

ברך — Barak — bless

ידע — Yada — know

2. Identify the Root

What is the root?

ברכתי → _____

Answer:

ברך

3. Match the Meaning

ברכתי → _____

ברכה → _____

(I bless / she blesses)

4. Pattern Recognition

Which ending means "I"?

ברכתי

ברכה

ברך

Answer: _____

5. Build the Meaning

Translate:

ברכת

→ ______

6. Reading Practice

Read:

ברך

ברכה

ברכתי

7. Cumulative Review

Read aloud:

אב

בן

מלך

מים

ארץ

ברא

אלהים

שמע

ברך

ידע

8. Mini Verb Recognition

Which one means “she heard”?

שמע

שמעה

שמעתי

Answer: ______

9. Final Reading

Read:

יהוה יברכך

Yahuah Yabarakha

May Yahuah bless you

Final Expressions

יהוה יברכך

Yahuah Yabarakha

May Yahuah bless you

ברוך יהוה

Baruk Yahuah

Blessed is Yahuah

Daily Walk with Yahuah

A Guided Path — Lesson 20: Two Expressions to Know Yahuah

ידעתי את יהוה

Yadaati at Yahuah

I have known Yahuah

יהוה קרוב אלי

Yahuah qarob alay

Yahuah is near to me

Lesson Summary

After 20 lessons, the student can now:

- recognize Hebrew roots
- identify common biblical words
- understand basic sentence structure
- recognize simple verb forms
- begin to understand who performs the action

FINAL READING EXERCISE FROM THE TANAK

Yada Yahuah — ידע יהוה — Biblical Hebrew

Introduction

After completing the first twenty lessons of this course, the student has learned:

- the 22 letters of the Hebrew alphabet
- the final letters (Sofit)
- frequent words from the Tanak
- common prefixes
- the definite article
- foundational Hebrew roots

In this final exercise, the goal is to practice reading using real words from the Tanak.

It is recommended that the student:

- read each word slowly
- listen to the pronunciation audios
- repeat the words aloud
- review the exercises several times

Part 1 — Alphabet Recognition

Read all the letters of the Hebrew alphabet.

א

ב

ג

ד

ה

ו

ז

ח

ט
י
כ
ל
מ
נ
ס
ע
פ
צ
ק
ר
ש
ת

Repeat the alphabet several times aloud.

Part 2 — Word Recognition

Read the following words from the Tanak.

אב

Ab

Father

בן

Ban

Son

מלך

Malak

King

מים
Mayim
Water

ארץ
Arats
Earth / Land

שם
Sham (Shem)
Name

יום
Yom
Day

אלהים
Alohiym

יהוה
Yahuah

Repeat these words several times.

Part 3 — Word Breakdown

Separate the letters of the following words.
1
מלך
מ
ל

ר

2
מים
מ
י
ם

3
ארץ
א
ר
ץ

4
בן
ב
ן

Part 4 — Word Reconstruction

Complete the words.

1
מ _ ך
Answer:
מלך

2
מ _ ם
Answer:
מים

3

א _ ץ

Answer:

ארץ

4

ב _

Answer:

בן

Part 5 — Prefix Recognition

Look at the following words.

ומלך

What is the prefix?

Answer:

ו = Wa = and

בארץ

What is the prefix?

Answer:

ב = Ba = in

למלך

What is the prefix?

Answer:

ל = La = for / to

Part 6 — Reading Phrases

Read the following phrases.

מלך ישראל

Malak Yasharal

King of Yasharal (Israel)

בן האדם
Ban HaAdam
Son of man

ברא אלהים
Bara Alohiym
Alohiym created

Part 7 — Reading Verses
Now we will read short phrases that appear in the Tanak.

Text
זה היום
Course transliteration:
Zah HaYom
Meaning:
This is the day
(Psalm 118:24)

Text
שמע ישראל
Transliteration:
Shama Yasharal
Meaning:
Hear, O Yasharal (Israel)

Part 8 — Reading the First Verse of the Tanak
Read the following text slowly.
בראשית ברא אלהים את השמים ואת הארץ

Course Transliteration

Barashit Bara Alohiym At HaShamayim WaAt HaArats

Meaning

In the beginning Alohiym created the heavens and the earth.

Verse Analysis

בראשית

Barashit

In the beginning

ברא

Bara

Created

אלהים

Alohiym

השמים

HaShamayim

The heavens

הארץ

HaArats

The earth

Part 9 — Final Reading

Read the following text in full:

בראשית ברא אלהים את השמים ואת הארץ

Repeat it aloud five times.

FINAL REFLECTION

If the student is able to read this verse and recognize several of its words, it means that the student has already developed the foundational skills needed to begin reading Biblical Hebrew.
This is the first step toward the purpose of the course:
ידע יהוה
Yada Yahuah
To know Yahuah.

Recommendation

Before continuing to Level 3, it is recommended that the student:
- review the alphabet
- repeat the reading exercises
- listen to the pronunciation audios
- read Genesis 1:1 again

Consistent practice will allow the student to recognize more and more words within the text of the Tanak.

The Most Frequent Words of the Tanak

Yada Yahuah — ידע יהוה — Biblical Hebrew
This list presents some of the words that appear most frequently in the Hebrew text of the Scriptures.
Learning these words allows the student to recognize a large portion of the Tanak much more quickly.
Each word includes:
- Hebrew text
- the course transliteration
- meaning
- Strong number

1 — Very Frequent Particles

These words appear thousands of times in the Tanak.

HEBREW	TRANSLITERATION	MEANING	STRONG
ו	Wa	And	—
את	At (et)	marker of the direct object	—
אל	Al (El)	toward / to	H413
על	Al	upon / over	H5921
מן	Min	From	H4480
כי	Ki	because / that	H3588
אם	Im	If	H518
לא	Lo	No	H3808
כל	Kol	all	H3605
אשר	Ashar	who / which / that	H834

2 — Very Common Nouns

HEBREW	TRANSLITERATION	MEANING	STRONG
אדם	Adam	man	H120
איש	Ish	man / male	H376
בן	Ban	son	H1121
אב	Ab	father	H1
מלך	Malak	king	H4428
עם	Am	people	H5971
ארץ	Arats	earth / land	H776
יום	Yom	day	H3117
מים	Mayim	water	H4325
שם	Sham (Shem)	name	H8034

3 — Words Related to Alohiym

HEBREW	TRANSLITERATION	MEANING	STRONG
אלהים	Alohiym	Alohiym	H430
יהוה	Yahuah	Name of the Creator	—
קדש	Qadash	to sanctify	H6942
ברך	Barak	to bless	H1288

4 — Very Frequent Verbs

HEBREW	TRANSLITERATION	MEANING	STRONG
ברא	Bara	to create	H1254
אמר	Amar	to say	H559
עשה	Asah	to do / make	H6213
נתן	Natan	to give	H5414
הלך	Halak	to walk	H1980
ראה	Raah	to see	H7200
שמע	Shama	to hear	H8085
ידע	Yada	to know	H3045
שמר	Shamar	to keep / guard	H8104
ישב	Yashab	to dwell	H3427

5 — Words Often Used in Biblical Phrases

SINGULAR	PLURAL	MEANING
בראשית	Barashit	in the beginning
ישראל	Yasharal (Yisrael)	Israel
שמים	Shamayim	heavens
הארץ	HaArats	the earth

Recognition Exercise

Read the following words:

בן

Ban

Son

מלך

Malak

King

ארץ

Arats

Earth / Land

יום

Yom

Day

מים

Mayim

Water

Reading Exercise

Read the phrase:

שמע ישראל

Transliteration:

Shama Yasharal

Meaning:

Hear, O Israel

Tanak Reading Exercise

Text:

בראשית ברא אלהים את השמים ואת הארץ

Transliteration:

Barashit Bara Alohiym At HaShamayim WaAt HaArats

Meaning:

In the beginning Alohiym created the heavens and the earth.

Study Recommendation

To learn these words, it is recommended that the student:

• read each word several times

• listen to the pronunciation audios

• repeat the words aloud

• try to recognize them inside the biblical text

Recognizing these words will allow the student to identify many phrases in the Tanak much more quickly.

Important Note

A student who knows:

• the Hebrew alphabet

• basic Hebrew roots

• these frequent words

can begin to recognize approximately 60–70% of many phrases in the Tanak. This makes it possible to move forward toward direct reading of the biblical text.

Guide to Reading the Tanak

Example: Genesis 1:1

After completing the first levels of Yada Yahuah — **ידע יהוה** — Biblical Hebrew, the student already has the essential tools needed to begin reading the Hebrew text of the Scriptures.

To illustrate this process, we will analyze one of the best-known verses in the Tanak: Genesis 1:1.

Hebrew Text

בראשית ברא אלהים את השמים ואת הארץ

Course Transliteration

Barashit Bara Alohiym At HaShamayim WaAt HaArats

Meaning

In the beginning Alohiym created the heavens and the earth.

Word-by-Word Analysis

HEBREW	TRANSLITERATION	MEANING	STRONG
בראשית	Barashit	in the beginning	H7225
ברא	Bara	created	H1254
אלהים	Alohiym	Alohiym	H430
את	At	direct object marker	—
השמים	HaShamayim	the heavens	H8064
ואת	WaAt	and (direct object marker)	—
הארץ	HaArats	the earth	H776

Observations

This verse contains several elements the student has already studied in the course.

Prefix

ו

Wa

and

Example:

ואת

WaAt

and

Definite Article
ה
Ha
the
Example:

השמים
HaShamayim
the heavens

Hebrew Root
ברא
Bara
to create
This verb appears frequently when the Tanak describes the creative action of Alohiym.

How to Read a Verse from the Tanak

To begin reading the Hebrew text of the Scriptures, it is recommended to follow these steps:

1. Read the Hebrew text.
2. Read the transliteration.
3. Listen to the pronunciation audio.
4. Analyze each word individually.
5. Understand the structure of the phrase.

With steady practice, the student will be able to recognize more and more words within the biblical text.

PREPARATION FOR LEVEL 3

In Level 3 of the course, the student will begin working more directly with the text of the Tanak, analyzing complete verses and expanding vocabulary.
The goal will be to learn how to:

• identify Hebrew roots
• recognize grammatical structures
• understand the meaning of words within their context

In this way, the student will continue advancing toward the purpose expressed in the name of this course:
ידע יהוה
Yada Yahuah
To know Yahuah.

The Yada Yahuah Method for Reading the Tanak
Yada Yahuah — **ידע יהוה** — Biblical Hebrew
After completing the first levels of this course, the student already possesses the essential tools needed to begin reading the Hebrew text of the Scriptures.
However, facing the text of the Tanak directly can seem difficult at first. The phrases may appear complex, and many words may still be unfamiliar.
For that reason, this course presents a simple method for analyzing any Hebrew verse.

This method is called:
The Yada Yahuah Method
Its purpose is to help the student approach the Hebrew text in an orderly and understandable way.

Step 1 — Read the Hebrew Text

The first step is simply to read the full Hebrew text.
It is not necessary to understand everything immediately.
The goal is to become familiar with the shape of the words.
Example

בראשית ברא אלהים את השמים ואת הארץ

Read the text slowly several times.

Step 2 — Identify Known Words

After reading the verse, the student should identify the words already learned.
For example, in this verse several words have already appeared in the course:

ברא
Bara
To create

אלהים
Alohiym

הארץ
HaArats
The earth

When the student recognizes some of the words, the verse immediately becomes more understandable.

Step 3 — Identify Prefixes and Articles

Biblical Hebrew uses prefixes that modify the meaning of words.
Some of the most common prefixes are:

ו — Wa — and
ב — Ba — in
ל — La — for / to
ה — Ha — the

Example from the verse

הארץ

Prefix:

ה

Ha

Meaning:

the earth

Recognizing these elements makes reading much easier.

Step 4 — Identify the Hebrew Root

Many Hebrew words are built from roots of three consonants.

Recognizing these roots helps the student understand the general meaning of many words.

Example

ברא

Root:

ב ר א

Central meaning:

to create

When the student recognizes the root, it becomes easier to understand the action described in the verse.

Step 5 — Understand the Structure of the Phrase

Biblical Hebrew often uses a word order different from English.

A very common order is:

Verb → Subject ⟶ Object

Example

ברא אלהים

ברא

Created

אלהים

Alohiym
Meaning:
Alohiym created

Understanding this order helps the student interpret the text correctly.

Applying the Method

Let us apply the full method to Genesis 1:1.
Text:
בראשית ברא אלהים את השמים ואת הארץ

1 — Read the Text

Read the complete verse several times.

2 — Identify Known Words

ברא
to create
אלהים
Alohiym
הארץ
the earth

3 — Identify Prefixes

ה
Ha
Example:
הארץ
the earth

4 — Identify Roots

ברא
to create

5 — Understand the Phrase

ברא אלהים

Alohiym created

Result

After applying these steps, the student can understand the verse:

בראשית ברא אלהים את השמים ואת הארץ

Meaning:

In the beginning Alohiym created the heavens and the earth.

Recommendation for the Student

To learn how to read the Tanak more easily, it is recommended to:

- read the verses several times
- listen to the pronunciation audios
- identify known words
- analyze Hebrew roots
- recognize prefixes and articles

With steady practice, the student will begin to recognize more and more words within the Hebrew text.

THE FINAL PURPOSE OF THE COURSE

Learning Biblical Hebrew is not simply a matter of memorizing words or grammatical rules.
The real goal is to approach the language in which the Scriptures were preserved.
For this reason, the name of the course summarizes its purpose:
ידע יהוה
Yada Yahuah
To know Yahuah.

COURSE GLOSSARY

Yada Yahuah — **ידע יהוה** — Biblical Hebrew
This glossary gathers the Hebrew words used throughout the lessons of the course.
It serves as a quick reference so that the student can review the vocabulary learned.
Each entry includes:
• the Hebrew word
• its transliteration
• its meaning
• the Strong number when applicable

Hebrew — English Glossary

HEBREW	TRANSLITERATION	MEANING	STRONG
אב	Ab	Father	H1
אבי	Abi	My father	—
איש	Ish	Man	H376
אלף	Alaf	Thousand	H505
אלהים	Alohiym (Elohiym)	God / gods	H430
את	At	Direct object marker	—
בארץ	BaArats	In the earth / land	—
בן	Ban	Son	H1121
בנים	Baniym	Sons	—
ברא	Bara	To create	H1254
בראשית	Barashit	In the beginning	H7225
דוד	Dawid	David	H1732
הארץ	HaArats	The earth / land	—
האיש	HaIsh	The man	—
היום	HaYom	The day	—
היה	Hayah	To be / to exist	H1961
והיה	WaHayah	And it shall be / and it was	—
והארץ	WaHaArats	And the earth	—
ומלך	WaMalak	And king	—
יד	Yad	Hand	H3027
יום	Yom	Day	H3117
ימים	Yamiym	Days	—
יהוה	Yahuah	Name of the Creator	—
ישראל	Yasharal (Yisrael)	Israel	—
כתב	Katab	To write	H3789
כתבים	Katabiym	Writings	H3791
כל	Kol	All / everything	H3605
למלך	LaMalak	To the king / for the king	—
מלך	Malak	King	H4428

HEBREW	TRANSLITERATION	MEANING	STRONG
מלכים	Malakiym	Kings	—
ממלכה	Mamlakah	Kingdom	H4467
מים	Mayim	Water	H4325
נח	Noach	Noah	H5146
נתן	Natan	To give	H5414
פרי	Pari (peri)	Fruit	H6529
צדיק	Tsadiq	Righteous	H6662
ציון	Tsiyon	Zion	H6726
ראה	Raah	To see	H7200
שמר	Shamar	To keep / observe	H8104
שמע	Shama	To hear / listen	H8085
שם	Sham	Name	H8034
ארץ	Arats	Earth / land	H776

How to Use the Glossary

To make the best use of this glossary, it is recommended that the student:

- look up the word whenever it appears in a lesson
- read the transliteration
- listen to the corresponding audio
- repeat the word aloud

Regular vocabulary review will help the student recognize words in the text of the Tanak more easily.

CONCLUSION

After completing the first two levels of Yada Yahuah — **ידע יהוה** — Biblical Hebrew, the student will have acquired a solid foundation for beginning to recognize and read the Hebrew text of the Scriptures.

Throughout these lessons, the fundamental elements of the language have been introduced, including:

- the 22 letters of the Hebrew alphabet
- the final letter forms (Sofit)
- common prefixes and particles
- the definite article
- foundational Hebrew roots
- frequent words from the Tanak
- basic elements of Hebrew sentence structure

With this knowledge, the student can begin recognizing many words within the biblical text and understanding how phrases are formed in Hebrew.
The next step will be to continue to Level 3, where the primary focus will be direct reading of the Tanak, analyzing verses word by word.
The ultimate purpose of this course is for the student to approach the Hebrew text of the Scriptures and continue deepening their understanding of the words that carry the original message.
In this way, learning the language also becomes a way of fulfilling the purpose expressed in the name of this course:
ידע יהוה
Yada Yahuah
To know Yahuah.

Course Digital Resources

Yada Yahuah — ידע יהוה — Biblical Hebrew

This course includes digital resources designed to complement the study of Biblical Hebrew and facilitate direct access to the text of the Scriptures. Students may use these tools to listen to the pronunciation of words, study the Hebrew text of the Tanak, and continue progressing in their learning of the language.

Website:

www.yahuahbible.com

Yahuah Bible Application

The Yahuah Bible app allows students to study the text of the Scriptures and analyze Hebrew words directly within the Tanak.

Its main features include:

- reading the biblical text
- access to the Strong concordance
- identification of Hebrew words
- searching for words within the Tanak
- comparing different biblical passages

This tool allows students to study Biblical Hebrew directly from the text of the Scriptures.

Available on:

- Android
- iOS
- Web (PWA) – pwa.yahuahbible.com

Pronunciation Audios

All Hebrew words and expressions included in this course have MP3 pronunciation audio available.

These audios allow the student to:

- hear the correct pronunciation of each word

• repeat the words aloud
• become familiar with the sound of Biblical Hebrew

It is recommended to listen to each audio several times and repeat the pronunciation in order to reinforce learning.

Supplementary Materials

In addition to the content of this book, the course may include additional materials such as:

• practice exercises
• vocabulary lists
• Tanak verse analysis
• Level 3 course material
• Student workbook

These resources help the student continue developing their understanding of Biblical Hebrew.

How to Use These Resources

To gain the greatest benefit from these digital tools, it is recommended that the student:

• study one lesson at a time
• listen to the corresponding audios
• repeat the words aloud
• practice reading the Hebrew text regularly

Consistent use of these tools will help the student recognize more and more words within the Tanak.

We'll meet again at Level 3 of Yada Yahuah — **ידע יהוה** — Biblical Hebrew

www.ingramcontent.com/pod-product-compliance
Lightning Source LLC
LaVergne TN
LVHW080333110826
845155LV00027B/235

* 9 7 8 1 9 4 6 2 4 9 4 2 5 *